Piano Time Piece.

GW00702752

EY SIGNATURE = Bb   KEY = Fmajor
ME   " = 4/4   Play Fmajor scale

Alexander march

Karl Czerny
(1791-1857)

13.11.97

Printed in Great Britain

Silent night

Franz Grüber
(1787-1863)
arr. Pauline Hall

Two contrasting pieces

In pencil, add your own fingering to these pieces.
In the first one you might try improvising. Keep the left hand the same,
but experiment with some different rhythms in the right hand.

Lonely trumpet

Balis Novak

A fifteenth-century tune

French folk-tune arr. Pauline Hall

Adagio = slow

Two tunes that are fun to sing and play

Somebody's knocking at your door

American singing game
arr. Pauline Hall

Some-bo - dy's knock-ing at your door, ___

Some-bo - dy's knock-ing at your door, ___

Oh, ___ Pe - ter Smith why don't you ans - wer?

Some-bo - dy's knock-ing at your door. ___

Frog went a-courting

American folk-song
arr. Pauline Hall

I hear a guitar

Hansi Alt

Waltzing Matilda

Australian song
arr. Pauline Hall

Gypsy tango

Gerald Martin

Moderately, with marked rhythm

Count your pennies

John Longmire

The Princess and the spinning-wheel

Pauline Hall

As the princess sits spinning she dreams about dancing a waltz at a grand ball. Make your playing tell the story.

Slowly and dreamily

Russian carol

arr. Pauline Hall

This carol should sound very bright and crisp.

A rainy-day round

A round is a song where the singers start, one after another, with the same tune. Your hands pretend to be the singers here. A third part is added for an extra hand.

arr. Pauline Hall

The little hedgehog

Notice that your left hand plays in the treble clef. You only need to use
fingers 1, 3 and 5 in both hands. When thumbs play, they are always on
next-door notes.
Listen for the prickles – on the first quaver of every bar – ouch!

There are only three chords in this piece:

Dmitri Kabalevsky

My bonnie lies over the ocean

arr. Pauline Hall

With a slow lilt

Prehistoric Piano Time

GREAT MUSIC + GREAT PICTURES = GREAT FUN!

Packed with fabulous dinosaur pieces, lively full-colour illustrations, games, and puzzles, *Prehistoric Piano Time* **is the most irresistible collection since the dawn of time!**

£4.95

For pupils of about Piano Time 1–2 standard

Become a super sight-reader!

Navigate the perilous path towards fluent sight-reading with confidence, using only your ten fingers, your wits, and these superb new sight-reading books from Pauline Hall to guide you.

The *Piano Time Sight-reading* books are enormous fun — guaranteed to improve every pupil's sight-reading. Using material which is simple, imaginative, and clearly laid out, Pauline Hall guides you step-by-step towards Grade 1 standard and beyond.

3 books — £3.95 each

Have you seen *Fun for Ten Fingers?*

'a breath of fresh air for teachers and pupils alike.'

21 pieces in five-finger position — all with humorous words and delightful illustrations.

The Oxford Piano Method

Starting out

Tunes for Ten Fingers	£4.25
More Tunes for Ten Fingers	£4.25
Fun for Ten Fingers	£4.25

Stage 1

Piano Time 1	£5.25
Piano Time Pieces 1	£5.25
Duets with a Difference	£5.25

Stage 2

Piano Time 2	£5.25
Piano Time Pieces 2	£5.25
Mixed Doubles (duets)	£5.25

Stage 3

Piano Time 3	£5.25
Piano Time Pieces 3	£5.25

More pieces to play

Piano Time Classics	£5.25
More Piano Time Classics	£5.25
Piano Time Carols	£4.95
Prehistoric Piano Time	£4.95

Sight-reading books

Piano Time Sight-reading 1	£3.95
Piano Time Sight-reading 2	£3.95
Piano Time Sight-reading 3	£3.95

Coming soon:

Piano Time Opera
Piano Time Jazz
Spooky Piano Time

Practice Makes Perfect

Full of useful advice, simple tunes and exercises, practice tips, listening games, and projects, *Practice Makes Perfect* includes something for everyone.
£5.25
Suitable for pupils of Grade 1–4 standard

Oxford Piano Method volumes are available at your local music shop, but if you have difficulty obtaining them please ring our distribution centre on 01536 741519.

✂ -

Would you like to be on our mailing list?

Please complete this form, put it in an envelope (no stamp required), and send it to **Music Department, Oxford University Press, FREEPOST, Oxford OX2 6BR**. We will send you details of new publications in the Oxford Piano Method series, the Oxford Music Bulletin twice a year, and future editions of the Oxford Keyboard Catalogue.

Name:

Address:

10 4202 11686

Menuetto

G.F. Handel
(1685–1759)
ed. Pauline Hall

'Menuetto' is the same as 'Minuet'.

Tarantella

Pauline Hall

A Tarantella is a fast, whirling dance from Sicily. Dancing it was
supposed to cure the bite of a tarantula.

Rattlesnake rag

Pauline Hall

No hurry – take this very steadily.

Play and Sing

The next pieces are songs for you to sing as you play. The left hand is the
accompaniment, so try to make it play more quietly than the right hand,
which plays the tune.

The wild buckaroo

arr. Pauline Hall

You can't keep a horse in a lighthouse

Clarges/Hill/Little
arr. Pauline Hall

You can't keep a horse in a light - house, it is-n't a

home for old Ned, _____ A hor - se's home is on dry

land, he'll ne-ver keep health-y on sea-foam and sand, Oh, you can let him

graze in the gar - age If you give him his meals on a

tray, _____ But you can't keep a horse in a light - house,

Neigh! Neigh! Neigh! _____

One more river

arr. Pauline Hall

You will have to fit the rhythm to the words of the second and third verses. You might like to have a go at making up some more verses of your own.

One more ri – ver, ___ and that's the ri – ver of Jor – dan,

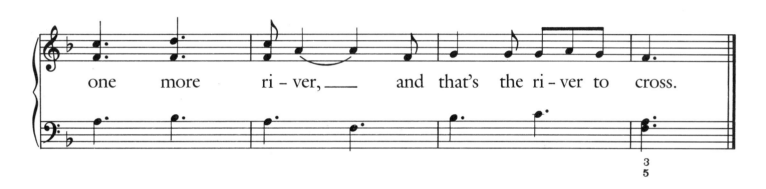

one more ri – ver, ___ and that's the ri – ver to cross.

2. The animals went in two by two,
   There's one more river to cross;
   The elephant and the kangaroo,
   There's one more river to cross,
   One more river, *etc.*

3. The animals went in three by three,
   There's one more river to cross;
   The lion, the mouse and the bumble-bee,
   There's one more river to cross,
   One more river, *etc.*

Alabama bound

American railroad ballad
arr. Pauline Hall

In the two bars where your left hand needs to move, there are rests, to give you the time to move up or down.

Steadily

pp

I'm Al-a-ba-ma bound, I'm Al-a-ba-ma bound, I'm Al-a-ba-ma bound, I'm Al-a-ba-ma bound, and if the train don't stop and turn a-round I'm Al-a-ba-ma bound, I'm Al-a-ba-ma bound.

pp

Gigue

Olive J. Wood

Allegretto in G

At the end you will find a triplet –

Fit these three notes evenly into one ♩ beat.

Joseph Haydn
(1732–1809)
ed. Maisie Aldridge

A ship a-sailing

Joan Last

Homeward bound

Pauline Hall

To help you with the rhythm, play this little exercise:

Valse triste

Robert Washburn

Although there seem to be a lot of flats about, this isn't a difficult piece. It
needs to go quite slowly to give your left hand time to swing over the
right. Put the sustaining pedal down and lift it up where it is marked.

Reproduced and printed by
Halstan & Co. Ltd., Amersham, Bucks., England

Acknowledgements

Illustrations by John Taylor

Thanks are due to the following for permission to reproduce copyright material:

Bosworth & Co. Ltd., London, for 'Count your Pennies' (J. Longmire), © 1966.

Forsyth Brothers Ltd., 126 Deansgate, Manchester M3 2GR, for 'Lonely Trumpet' (B. Novak) from *Feelin' Good*.

EMI Music Publishing Ltd. and International Music Publications, for 'You can't keep a horse in a lighthouse' (words and music by B. Clarges, J. Hill, and E. Littler). © 1937 B. Feldman & Co. Ltd., London WC2H 0LD.

Oxford University Press, for 'The Little Hedgehog' (D. Kabalevsky) from *Easy Russian Piano Music Book 2*, compiled by M. Aldridge, © OUP 1974; and *A Little Suite* (O. Wood), © OUP 1926.

Century Music Publishing Co., for *Gypsy Tango* (G. Martin), © 1964, all rights reserved.

Oxford University Press Inc., New York, for 'I hear a guitar' (H. Alt) from *Five Summer Sundays*, © 1974; and 'Valse Triste' (R. Washburn), © 1964.